Colossal Head of Zeus (1)
Hellenistic, 3rd—2nd century BC
Troy
(Inv. no 685, H. 55 cm)

(1)

ISTANBUL ARCHAEOLOGICAL MUSEUMS

ALPAY PASINLI

(Director of Istanbul Archaeological Museums)

A TURIZM YAYINLARI LTD·ISTANBUL

Front cover
Alexander Sarcophagus
Back cover
Istanbul Archaeological Museums. Exterior view and gardens

Editor
Fatih Cimok

Photographs
Suat Eman

Layout
Feryal Özbay

Filmset
Çali Grafik

Printers
Akbasım Matbaacılık Ltd.

Printed in Turkey
First printing May 1989
Second printing October 1992

Editor:
A Turizm Yayınları
Şifa Hamamı Sokak 18,
Sultanahmet, Istanbul 34400, Turkey
Tel. (1) 516 24 97; Fax. (1) 516 41 65

INTRODUCTION

The Istanbul Archaeological Museums complex is the most important of its kind in Turkey in respect to the number and value of its exhibits, and it can challenge some of the oldest and largest museums in the world. This complex comprises three separate museums. These are the Çinili Köşk or the "Tiled Pavilion" in which Turkish tiles and ceramics are on display, the Museum of the Ancient Orient, which houses mostly Hittite and Mesopotamian antiquities, and the Archaeological Museum with its artifacts of classical archaeology. In 1881 Osman Hamdi Bey was appointed to Çinili Köşk as the director of this Ottoman Imperial Museum, becoming at the same time the first Turkish museum director in the Ottoman Empire. The Archaeological Museum itself was founded by Osman Hamdi Bey and opened to the public on 13th June 1891 as an imperial museum. The Museum of the Ancient Orient however was founded as the Academy of Fine Arts in 1883 also by Osman Hamdi Bey.

Altogether these museums possess sixty thousand objects of archaeology, eight hundred and sixty thousand coins and similar artifacts, and seventy five thousand cuneiform tablets. These antiquities cover a wide range of history from 7th millenium BC to the 20th century AD.

The Ottoman Empire comprised almost all the lands which fall into the "Fertile Crescent" area, for different periods, from the early 16th century until the late 19th century. Among these lands, Egypt, Mesopotamia, Iraq, Iran and Anatolia had been the home of important civilizations since prehistoric times, and except for the activities of ancient treasure seekers or grave robbers, the soil of these lands hid the remains of these ancient cultures until the 18th century.

The interest of the European nations in archaeology began before the Ottoman interest in the subject, and they had little difficulty in obtaining permission from the Ottoman State, to look for and excavate ancient sites of archaeology. After this period and until the establishment of the modern Turkish Republic, these lands became a field of competition between the ambitious French, German and English adventurers and archaeological missions were often financed and supported by their governments. A very large proportion and some most important objects of antiquity displayed in the museums of these nations, were taken away from Ottoman lands during this period.

Although certain Ottoman sultans showed some individual interest in objects of antiquity, the interest of the Ottomans for modern archaeology did not start until the second half of the 19th century. The Oriental works of art displayed in modern Turkish museums, such as the Istanbul Archaeological Museums complex are either those discovered during hasty excavations, or were haphazardly gathered here and there until the outbreak of the First World War. At this date such lands officially broke away from the Ottoman Empire and modern states were established.

The Anatolian peninsula has been the luckiest of all the lands of the Fertile Crescent — this was confirmed just within the last sixty years — in regard to ancient civilizations. It was not merely a bridge between Asia and Europe by which groups of people migrated. Research has shown that some parts of the peninsula were occupied by palaeolithic hunters as early as 600,000 years before the present day. Later during the Neolithic and Chalcolithic eras, the Anatolian plateau created indigenous urban societies which were developed sufficiently enough to transmit their culture to the countries surrounding the peninsula. In a later period some of the settlements of these cultures would serve as home for new emigrants such as Hittites, Phrygians and Greeks. The ancient sites which all these civilizations left in Anatolian soil have been an immense cultural heritage for modern Turkey, and have supplied modern Turkish museums with continuous material. This is the very thing which distinguishes the museums of Turkey from the museums of other countries.

No single book can deal with a collection as large as the one which belongs to the Istanbul Archaeological Museums, and any selection which can be included in a publication must be arbitrary. Since it is the collection of royal sarcophagi — which is displayed in the Archaeological Museum — which has won the museum complex its fame, compared to the other objects of interest, these are dealt with at length in this publication. Also, at the time these lines were being written, a number of objects were about to be moved to the new premises, and this is the reason I have refrained from giving the exact location of each object.

This book is intended to assist visitors to better appreciate some of the works of art on display. All detailed information pertaining to these objects can be found in the works of the many scholars who have devoted their lives to their study. I am also indebted to my colleagues in various departments at the museums who willingly offered their specialized knowledge.

Alpay Pasinli

(2)

4

ARCHAEOLOGICAL MUSEUM

Historical records indicate that the interest of Turks for art works of antiquity goes back to the thirteenth century. It is known that the Seljuk sultan Alaaddin Keykubat (1220—35) decorated the fortifications of his capital, Konya (ancient Iconium), with Roman and Byzantine reliefs, statues and architectural fragments. The same interest must must have been cultivated by some of the Ottoman sultans as well. Plenty of Christian relics and important works of antiquity, such as the red porphyry sarcophagi and the base of the monument of the fourth century AD charioteer Porphyrius — both in the Archaeological Museum — owe their survival to the interest of Sultan Mehmet II, the Conqueror, in ancient works of art. Nevertheless, the earliest systematic attempt to collect and preserve ancient works of art began during the reign of Sultan Abdülmecit (1839—61). At this date the antiquities sent from various parts of the large Ottoman Empire were collected and stored in the former Church of Hagia Eirene, at that time used as an arsenal for old weaponry. Towards the end of the century these antiquities were moved to the Çinili Köşk.

Today, the Archaeological Museum constitutes the main building of the museum complex, and owes its existence to the group of sarcophagi which came from a royal necropolis at Sidon (Sayda) in 1887. Until then the Çinili Köşk was used as a museum. However, the discovery of such a large collection made the construction of a new building imperative. When these sarcophagi were brought to the capital through Osman Hamdi Bey's efforts, the present building was constructed and opened to the public on 13th June 1891. This discovery was one of the most spectacular archaeological events of the nineteenth century, and after it was inaugurated, for a while this new museum was known as the "Museum of Sarcophagi". The sarcophagi which were then moved into this building are still on display at the points where they were originally placed. Later, in order to accommodate other findings, two additional wings were added in 1902 and 1908 and the museum took its present form. The important architectural elements of its design were inspired by the Alexander Sarcophagus and the Sarcophagus of Mourning Women, and to these, various features of architecture of antiquity were added.

At present, the collection of the museum numbers some forty five thousand pieces: nine thousand of these are stone objects, twelve thousand are pieces of pottery of various kinds, ten thousand are terracotta (mainly figurines), ten thousand metal and three thousand glass objects. Due to the shortage of space only a small portion of this collection can be displayed. While the stone objects belonging to Greek, Roman and Byzantine civilizations are being displayed in the twenty halls of the ground floor, the rooms on the first floor serve to exhibit the terracotta, glass, pottery, and other kinds of small antiquities. However, at the time this volume was written, preparation was under way to move a large part of the small objects to the new premises, where they can be displayed using a more modern and spacious style of presentation, thus ensuring easier study of the exhibits from every angle.

A few words are necessary on the museum library as well. The museum library is located on the first floor of the left wing, and occupies an area of about 400 sq m. It was founded at the same time as the museum, and houses approximately seventy thousand books, covering a wide range of subjects, including archaeology, history, fine arts, military tactics, geography and literature. There are about two thousand hand-written volumes. The interior architecture of the library, as well as its classic furniture, may be equalled by only a few libraries in the world.

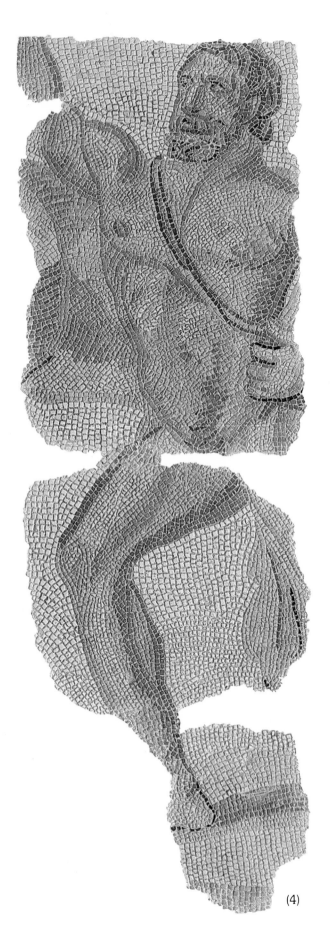

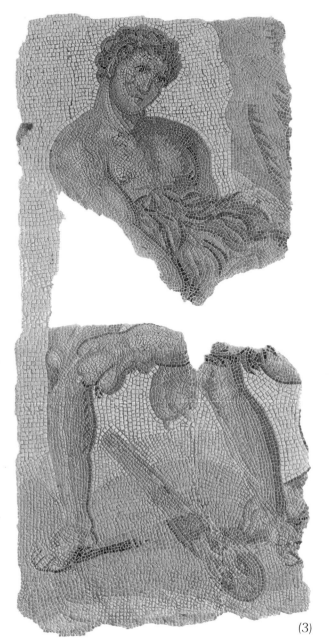

(3)

(4)

Herakles killing the Nemean Lion (3)
Roman, 2nd—3rd century AD
Edessa (Urfa), Birecik
(Inv. no 2464, H. 153 cm, W. 71.5 cm)

A young and beardless Herakles is depicted strangling the Lion sent by the goddess Hera to ravage Nemea in the Peloponnese with his bare hands (the first labour). On the ground his club is seen.

Herakles Stealing the Apples of the Hesperides (4)
Roman, 2nd—3rd century AD
Edessa (Urfa), Birecik
(Inv. no 2466, H. 153.5 cm, W. 54 cm)

Atlas is depicted in the Gardens of the Hesperides about to pluck the apples for Herakles (the eleventh labour).

PAINTED STELAE OF SIDON

Painted stelae of Sidon are among the most interesting remains of the popular arts executed in Syria during the Hellenistic period. Their popularity must have been a result of the fondness of the Sidonians for painted decorations as well as a scarcity of good quality marble for producing sculpture. Similar stelae were also excavated in Cyprus and Egypt. Those at the Archaeological Museum of Istanbul belonged to Greek mercenaries who served in the armies of the Seleucid kings, and they give us valuable information about the arms and apparel of soldiers recruited by the Seleucids in the second century BC.

Funeral Stele of Salmamodes (?) (5)
Hellenistic, 2nd century BC
Sidon (Sayda)
(Inv. no 1167, H. 86 cm, W. 48.5 cm)

Funeral Stele of Dioscurides of Balboura (6)
Hellenistic, 2nd century BC
Sidon (Sayda)
(Inv. no 1490, H. 111 cm, W. 56 cm)

An armed soldier is represented in combat position at the centre of a deep niche. He advances towards the left, while a triangular sword is seen in his raised right hand. His left hand carries a large oval shield. A plumed helmet protects his head. His laced shoes reach to his ankles. All over the surface of the stele, paint was applied over a white coating and some of this paint still survives. The niche is surmounted by an architrave and a triangular pediment carrying a triple acroteria.

(6)

Previous pages: **Sarcophagus of Sidamara** (7)

Sidamara-type Sarcophagus (8)
Roman, 2nd—3rd century AD
Nicea (Iznik), Ömerli Village
(Inv. no 5123, H. 156 cm, L. 230 cm, W. 126 cm)

SARCOPHAGUS
OF SIDAMARA

Sarcophagus of Sidamara (7)
Roman, first half of 3rd century AD
Sidamara (Konya, Ambararası)
(Inv. no 1179, H. 313 cm, L. 381 cm, W. 200 cm)

This sarcophagus is known as the finest and most important specimen of this group of sarcophagi which are named after it. The columns and placing of the figures between the columns on the casket of this particular sarcophagus bring to mind the "column sarcophagi", and especially the Sarcophagus of Mourning Women, which outdates it by some six hundred years. The faces of the casket are treated like the surface of a wall. On the principal side six fluted columns create a triangular niche at the centre and two arched niches at each side of it. The niches are decorated with drilled foliage decoration which frequently includes eggs and dentils as well. This decoration fills the areas outside the niches and continues on the other sides of the casket. At the centre of this rather complicated architecture the royal personage to whom the sarcophagus belongs is shown seated on a chair. He is depicted with the conventional drapery, physiognomy and pose of a philosopher. While his right hand rests on the lion pelt covering his seat his other hand holds a book. His figure is too big for the niche reserved for him, and to fit him into space, the sculptor has had to stretch his right leg awkwardly into the adjoining niche. On the right his wife is represented. Her head turns towards her dead husband. Her eyes are not incised. The over-all rough sculpturing indicates hasty work. On the other side a young girl is shown also her head turned towards the central figure. She must be the daughter of the dead person, and is represented in the attire of the goddess Artemis. The two Dioscuri flank the family on both sides. Each of them is dressed only in a chlamys secured on their shoulders by a round buckle. Their legs are too short for their bodies. Each holds a long lance in one hand and the reins of a horse — sacrificial animal — in the other.

On the top of the lid the person to whom the sarcophagus belongs and his wife are depicted in a half-reclining pose. Both of them are crudely sculpted and

have been damaged. The lid is surrounded by a band of relief decorated with putti or Erotes hunting animals, and wild animals fighting among themselves.

On the second long side of the casket a hunting scene is depicted. Five young men mounted on horses are shown hunting various kinds of animals. Their odd number prevented the artist employing an exactly symmetric distribution, and thus their horses had to be rendered in profile. The narrow band of frieze at the bottom of this composition is regarded as the best part of the sarcophagus. Although it contains stereotype motifs of the era to which it belongs, it deserves emphasis for the simplicity, realistic character and skilful rendering of its figures.

On one of the short sides of the casket a door — the door of a tomb — is seen at the centre of a niche. From the left side a young woman approaches the door carrying a container from which she seems to pick some figs or grapes. The bearded man on the opposite side is seen holding a scroll.

On the other short side a single young man is seen mounted and hunting assisted by his dogs. The narrow frieze below this scene shows various compositions depicting chariot races.

Archaeologists do not regard the "Sidamara sarcophagi" as an independent type or an isolated group. They have affinities with the sarcophagi produced before them and with those produced at the same period. Their originality probably lies in the fact that these sarcophagi bring together two kinds of the most common types of grave monuments: those which show the dead in half-reclining pose on a couch, and those sculpted like houses or temples. Excessive use of the drill which often distorted the figures, is very common for the Sidamara sarcophagi. Although the original home of Sidamara-type sarcophagi has not yet been established, its frequent appearance in Anatolia seems to suggest an Anatolian origin.

(8)

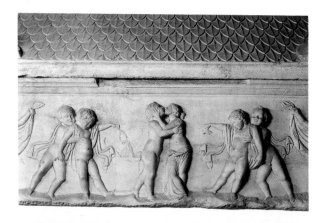

Sarcophagus Decorated with Putti (9)
Roman, 2nd century AD
Thessalonica
(Inv. no 511, H. 142.5 cm, L. 205.5 cm, W. 95 cm)

The centre of the composition on the principal side of the casket shows a putto and a little girl — obviously inspired by common scenes between the Erotes and the Psyches — in an amorous embrace, with their mouths comically locked together. On their left a fire altar is placed. They are flanked by a pair of putti on each side; the drunk one falling into the arms of the more sober one. The drunk putto on the left throws a crown of flowers into the fire. The drunk one on the other side holds a small bird.

(10)

Funeral Stele of Gaios (10)
Roman, 3rd century AD
Kütahya or Altıntaş
(Inv. no 5, H. 123 cm, W. 63 cm)

The two busts portrayed in the lowest part of the stele resemble each other: big eyes, small mouths and ears, long thin fingers, similar attire and disposition. Above their heads a funeral inscription which extends to the surface of the pillar on the right is seen. In the middle part of the stele is the triple goddess Hecate. (In mythology she has three bodies, originally those of a lion, a dog and a mare.) Here each is shown as a young woman holding a torch. They are flanked by two gods. The god on their right is in a short tunic worked like armour. His hairstyle brings to mind a "Phrygian cap". The naked god on the other side is seen offering something like a bird to a dog with one hand and holding a double-axe in the other. Above the triple Hecate from left to right are an open diptych, the bust of Helios, a bird perched on a basket, a comb, and a mirror with handle. The acroterion of the stele consists of palmets of different sizes. At the centre of the pediment an eagle with open wings is placed. At the lowest part of the stele is a plough.

(11)

Funeral Banquet Stele (11)
Hellenistic, 3rd—1st century BC
Cyzicus (Erdek)
(Inv. no 11, H. 66.5 cm, L. 84.5 cm)

Four men are represented in half-reclining pose on a couch. Three of them hold cups in their left hands. In front of their couch a table with food — cake and grapes — and a crater are placed. They are flanked by a seated woman on each side. Four domestics are seen serving at a banquet. At the upper left corner a tree with a snake — with a forked tongue — is seen. At the other corner the profile of a horse's head is placed. The stele is inscribed at its lowest part.

(12)

Sarcophagus of Phaedra and Hippolytus
(12)
Roman, 2nd century AD
Tripoli (Syria)
(Inv. no 508, H. 162 cm, L. 209 cm, W. 111 cm)

The centre of the composition on the principal side of the casket is occupied by Hippolytus who is represented taller than the rest of the figures. His dress — like that of his two companions — is only a chlamys held on the shoulder with a round buckle. He carries a long javelin in his left hand and has a sword at this waist. In his right hand the diptych containing the love message from Phaedra — his stepmother — is seen. He looks toward the old servant who is seen waiting for her answer in front of him. Except for her peculiarly depicted large left hand, her figure shows strong individual characterization, and is probably from a Hellenistic model. Behind her, another servant is seen also eager to hear Hippolytus' answer. Phaedra is shown seated — rather noncholantly — in a chair. Her head is turned to the back as if trying to hear the servant better — seen behind her. The servant seems to whisper words of hope or consolation into the ear of her mistress. A small Eros is shown at the feet of Phaedra touching her knees. On this side the composition ends with a dog and a tree with leaves.

At the right part of the composition the two companions of the hero are shown. Like him they are about to depart for their hunting trip. The one on the left holds the horse of Hippolytus, not by its reins, but by some kind of long rope whose end must have been touching his knee. Traces of this on his knee have survived. His left hand holds his swordguard. The second young man carries a javelin in his left hand and holds a dog by its leash with the other. This side of the composition also ends with a tree.

At the two corners of the lid are placed two Erotes. The one on the left holds a big bunch of grapes in his hands. The other one has a fat bird, probably a goose.

Although this legend has been a subject for innumerable works of art, the sarcophagus is regarded as one of the finest samples. The surface of the marble is well-polished — a feature often encountered in the works of the second century — to give darker tones, thus creating a strong contrast to match the contrast created by the deeply drilled decoration — acanthus leaves, egg and tongue bands and astragal — of the lid.

Sarcophagus of Mourning Women (13)

Sarcophagus of Mourning Women (14)

THE SIDON COLLECTION

Sarcophagus of Mourning Women (15)

The group of sarcophagi which were discovered in 1887 at Sidon, is regarded as being among the most important works of classical archaeology. The necropolis was discovered accidentally by a villager while he was trying to dig a well. When news of the discovery reached Istanbul, Osman Hamdi Bey, who was the director of the museum at the time, went to Sidon and supervised the excavations personally.

The sarcophagi were placed in two underground burial chambers which were both insulated against humidity and water seepage. One of the rooms was robbed but the second one was still intact when discovered. After the excavations the finds were carried to the capital, and at the time this publication was being prepared, were still on display where they were originally put and are the major attraction of the museum. The most important of these sarcophagi are known by the names: Sarcophagus of Mourning Women, Alexander Sarcophagus, Satrap Sarcophagus, Lycian Sarcophagus and Tabnit Sarcophagus.

The result of later research suggests that these sarcophagi belonged to a group of fairly successive kings who ruled in Phoenicia, and were put into the burial vaults in their order of succession. The so-called Alexander Sarcophagus was probably the last one to be sculpted and placed in the burial chamber.

Sarcophagus of Mourning Women (16)

SARCOPHAGUS OF MOURNING WOMEN

Sarcophagus of Mourning women (13, 14, 15, 16, 17, 18)
Mid-4th century BC
Sidon (Sayda)
(Inv. no 368, H. 297 cm, L. 254 cm, W. 137 cm)

This sarcophagus is known as the finest example of a kind known as the "column sarcophagi". It should be seen not as a burial place but as a monumental tomb or a sacred last resting place such as the "Mausoleum" or the "Nereid" monument. Its Ionic architecture is repeated in the exterior architecture of the Archaeological Museum.

Originally the sarcophagus was painted and it still carries very slight traces of its colours. It is a Greek work of art, and Oriental influences are observed only in the long robes (chitons) worn by the figures, and in the chariots of the funeral corteges. The gestures of distress and wailing are those common for Semitic people as well as shorn heads, naked feet and torn clothing. The sarcophagus is thought to have belonged to King Straton of Sidon who died in 360 BC. The king was known as a man fond of the pleasures of Eros.

Eighteen women — not professional mourners common in the Orient, but connected persons — who must have been his wives or an actual part of his harem, are depicted mourning for their master. They are separated from each other by Ionic columns, and shown sitting or standing in different poses; some holding their heads, some their chins in various dispositions.

The idea of death and distress depicted on the casket is emphasized by the funeral corteges shown on the two long sides of the lid. Except for small changes in drapery and for the pose of the young men at the heads of both corteges, the two are identical: a young man, two young men leading horses — sacrificial animals —, a Persian quadriga with another young man to manage its four horses, a funeral cart — carrying a rectangular casket with a lid — led by another man, a bearded man leading a horse with a young men following behind. Compared to the work on the casket, the reliefs on the lid are of poor workmanship and were probably executed by a different and less skilful sculptor.

15

Sarcophagus of Mourning Women (17)

On one of the short sides of the casket three women are represented in similar attire, physiognomy and poses, with the rest of the figures on the other sides of the casket. The woman at the centre sits on the balustrade, which gives a depth to the faces of the casket and helps to avoid monotomy.

At the centre of the triangular pediment of the lid on this side a woman is seen sitting on the grave mound. Her feet like those of all the figures are bare. She is flanked by two younger women whose gestures and whose demeanour express deep and silent distress. One of them is seen leaning slightly on the grave mound.

On the right side of the frieze above the pediment, a bearded man is seen sitting on the ground. In front of him a younger man, one hand on his knee, the other extended towards the other, seems to be saying words of consolation. This frieze is repeated on the other side of the lid as well and they differ very slightly.

Sarcophagus of Mourning Women (18)

On the other short side of the casket the last three of the eighteen women are seen. They are almost the same as the others.

The way that the figures of the three wailing women are represented in the pediment is the reverse of those on the opposite side, differing slightly only in the drapery.

The reliefs of the frieze on the right side have not survived. On the left side an old man is shown sitting on the ground. His left hand supports his head. He extends his right hand in a gesture of address to the young man in front of him. The latter is seen holding his robe with one hand in the front and raising the other hand above his head as if trying to tear it or take it off in a gesture of deep sorrow. His action confirms the idea that the poses of the wailing figures on the sarcophagus are not taken from a stereotype art repertoire but from real life.

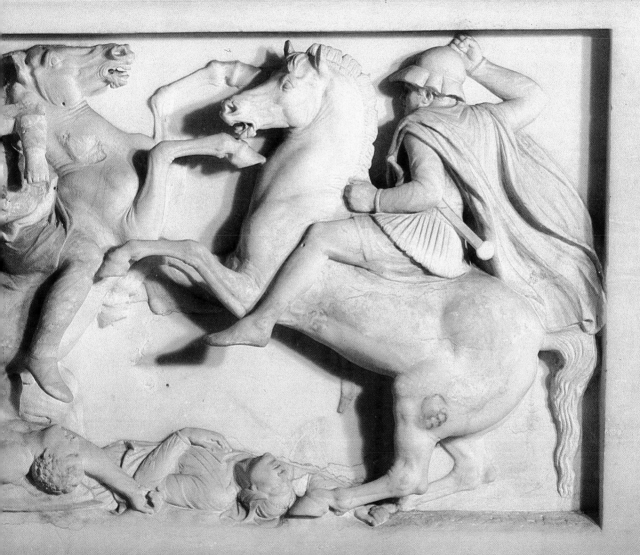

ALEXANDER SARCOPHAGUS

Alexander Sarcophagus (19, 20, 21, 22, 23, 24)
Late 4th century BC
Sidon (Sayda)
(Inv. no 370, H. 195 cm, L. 318 cm, W. 167 cm)

The Alexander Sarcophagus is known as the most important work of antiquity in the Archaeological Museum. It was discovered in 1887 in an underground royal necropolis at Sidon. It has arrived to the present in almost pristine condition, and the small amount of damage, as well as the absence of metal ornamentation such as lances or swords, must have been caused by the treasure seekers who robbed the burial chamber.

One one of the long sides of the casket a battle scene between the Persians and the Greeks is shown. While the Greeks wear short tunics or cloaks, the Persian soldiers are shown in long trousers (anaxyrides), long-sleeved shirts of several layers, and with tiaras covering their heads, all confirming to the Persian tradition of banning the display of men's flesh — except for the face and the tips of the fingers.

On the very left of the composition Alexander is seen mounted on a horse and chasing a Persian soldier. His headgear, the pelt of the Nemean Lion's head — the symbol of Herakles from whom he claimed descent — helps to distinguish him. (The coins issued by him at Sidon's mint also depict him as the young Herakles wearing this traditional trophy.) In addition, next to his ear there is a ram's horn, the symbol of the Egyptian god Amon. His raised right arm is in the act of hurling a spear. His horse has received an arrow in its shoulder; the right front leg shows ancient restoration. The horse is trampling on the dead body of a Persian. The horse of his enemy has fallen onto its forelegs. Its rider is trying to defend himself from Alexander with his raised sword held in his right hand. Next to this are two soldiers engaged in foot combat. The armoured Greek soldier, covering himself with a round shield, is about to drive his sword into his enemy, who has lost his weapons and raises his hands helplessly in an instinctive gesture of protection. One leg of the Greek soldier stands heedlessly on the fallen body of another Persian. In the central group a mounted Greek, while trying to manage his horse with his left hand, is about to give a killing blow

to a Persian soldier. The latter has lowered one knee to the ground and raised his shield to protect himself. His weaponless right arm touches the flank of the other's horse. Under the animal the dead body of a Persian — his tiara fallen from his head — is shown partly covered by his red-painted shield. In the left background a Persian soldier is shooting an arrow at Alexander. Next to them a mounted and armed Persian is charging a Greek. The tunic of the latter has fallen from his shoulders and left his body naked. His helmet has also gone. With his left hand he grasps the lower jaw of his adversary's horse and raises his sword against the other. In the foreground, another Persian who has kneeled on the ground is aiming an arrow at a mounted Greek commander who is placed at the far right-hand side. The Greek commander is charging at a Persian who is already dead and falling into the arms of one of his comrades. The latter has raised his shield to protect himself and his dead friend. Under the horses' hooves the corpses of a Greek and a Persian are seen.

It has been claimed that this battle scene must symbolize the battle of Issus (333 BC) which opened to Alexander the gates of Phoenicia and Syria. It was owing to this battle that the fortunes of Abdalonymos, to whom the sarcophagus is thought to have actually belonged, changed, and he became the King of Sidon.

On the second long face of the casket two hunting scenes, those of a lion and deer are depicted. This side is less crowded than the battle scene. A big lion occupies the centre of this composition. Although its body is pierced at several points and blood is seen gushing from these wounds, it has stuck its claws into the shoulders of the horse — depicted as rather indifferent to what is going on. The rider of this horse has raised his lance towards the wild animal. The use of horses and chariots in lion hunts is an Oriental tradition, and Alexander is known to have participated in such lion hunts in Phoenicia. This rider is thought to represent the Phoenician king Abdalonymos. In accordance with the

Next pages: **Alexander Sarcophagus** (20)

custom of the time he wears Persian attire. From both sides hunters run to his assistance. Behind the lion another Persian has raised his axe in both hands and is about to give a formidable blow to the head of the animal. Close to him a mounted Greek — in a symmetrical movement with that of the mounted Persian on the opposite side — raises his lance towards the lion. He is thought to represent Hephaestion, a general of Alexander's and his close friend. Under his horse a greyhound — altogether there are three greyhounds included in the scene — has stuck its teeth into the left hind leg of the wild animal. On the left-hand side Alexander, this time identified by a royal diadem — which has not survived but for its indentations — is represented. His idealized physiognomy and the disposition of his dress apply to other figures as well and do not help much to identify him. In his right hand he holds a lance and charges at the lion. Behind him a naked Greek rushes to the struggle. His chlamys is rolled around his left arm. The carving of his fingers indicates that he is armed with a lance in his left hand and an axe or a cutlass in the other. This figure is almost completely detached from the surface of the casket and regarded as one of the magnificent examples of Greek art of the period. Unfortunately the head has not survived. Behind him a Persian is seen releasing an arrow at the lion.

It is known that after capturing Persia, Alexander wanted to assimilate the Hellenistic and the Oriental worlds and create a Greco-Persian Empire. Towards the end of his life he married Persian princesses, wore Persian dress, and adopted the pomp and protocol of the Persian court. The presentation of the Persians and Greeks as friends participating in a hunt can be seen in this light. After defeating Darius (336—30 BC) at the battle of Issus (near today's Iskenderun), he crossed the Amanus mountains and, following the coast of the Mediterranean, invaded Syria. The inhabitants of Sidon who disliked Persian rule, opened the gates of their

prosperous city to the Macedonian army. Being discontented with their present ruler, they asked Alexander to appoint a king for their city. Alexander did not have enough time to choose a king for Sidon, and gave the task to Hephaestion. Abdalonymos was distantly related to the Sidonian royal house and lived a modest life outside the city. Hephaestion chose him as the King of Sidon. It is the same Abdalonymos — in Persian his name means "servant of gods" — who is claimed to have commissioned the Alexander Sarcophagus and included his benefactors, Alexander and Hephaestion in the reliefs.

At the far right side of this hunting scene another isolated hunting representation is placed. A Greek and a Persian are seen killing a deer. The flowing chlamys of the Greek leaves his body naked. While he pulls the head of the deer by its horns violently towards his side, he buries a javelin in its flank. On the other side the Persian hunter raises his axe with both hands in an attitude exactly the same as that of the Persian behind the lion, and is about to strike the animal.

The lid, as well as the casket of the sarcophagus, is made of Pentelic marble. The sarcophagus must have been produced at Sidon, because the risk of transporting such a delicate work of art for long distances would have been very high. Although the scenes are depicted in separate panels with borders, both the figural representations and the non-figural ones constitute a unity. There is no information about the identity of the sculptor. However, it is thought that he would not have been famous, as a well-known sculptor would not have accepted a commission where such a work would end in an underground burial chamber. The painters of the sarcophagus are thought to have been as skilful as the sculptor. Originally, the hair, eyes, eyelashes, lips and clothing of the figures were painted in violet, yellow, burnt sienna, blue, red and purple, while the flesh area was given only a slight lacquer.

Alexander Sarcophagus (21)

On one of the shorter sides of the casket a battle showing three isolated fighting scenes is represented. The central part shows a mounted Persian hurling his lance at a naked Greek fallen on the ground. The latter is weaponless. Traces of his fallen lance and helmet which were originally indicated in colour, survive. His muscled back and shoulders are clearly seen. He makes a last effort to defend himself with his shield. On the right side of this scene is a Greek killing a Persian. His chlamys is flowing over his left shoulder. With his left arm, which arries a shield, he violently pulls the head of his enemy to the back and stabs him with a dagger at the shoulder. The Persian is on his knees. The traces of his tiara, which must have fallen from his head during the struggle and is indicated in yellow paint, survive. While his left arm which bears his shield is helplessly thrown upwards, with his right hand he struggles against the enemy, holding him by his arm. In the last combat scene on the left, another naked Greek soldier is shown charging at his Persian enemy with a sword. The latter is taking a retreating step and trying to defend himself with his sword held in his right hand. Both soldiers carry circular shields like the rest of the fighters in the composition. Probably a single-unit effect has been sought after by using the same sort of shield, showing them at different angles while held in various attitudes. The original predominant red colour on this side of the casket has survived better than on the other sides. The shields which are carried by the Persians are painted on their inner sides with a design in the Persian manner. It has been claimed that this scene represents the battle of Gazze (312 BC) in which Abdalonymos was killed. It thus helps to date the sarcophagus as well.

On the other short side of the casket a panther hunt is depicted. All of the participants are Orientals. At the centre of the composition the master of the hunt is seen in the act of hurling a javelin at the panther. His left arm bears a circular shield. According to Xenophon, the shield to the Persians was a part of the hunting gear. The panther is depicted with the conventional features of the period. Its head is very small for its long neck. Its paws are too long. The forequarters of the body are also too big and the hindquarters too small. It is shown in an indecisive stage of action. Behind the animal three grooms of the hunter — one with an axe and the others with lances — are attacking the panther. At the other side another groom is seen trying to control the scared horse of his master. Under the horse a greyhound is shown. Its features lack detail.

The pediments of the lid also show fighting scenes. These reliefs compared to those on the casket, are of poor workmanship, and must have been sculpted by less skilful craftsmen.

The pediment on this side shows a fight between the Persians and the Greeks. It is interpreted as showing the soldiers of Abdalonymos fighting against the Greeks. At the centre of the composition a mounted Persian has raised his lance in a threatening attitude. In front of him and on the left of the scene a Greek soldier is placed. He wears armour but his head is unprotected. His legs are spread apart. He is armed with a sword in his right hand and with a small shield held in the left. In the background his fallen lance and helmet are indicated in colour. To the left of this another Persian is shown with one knee on the ground. His sword-bearing right arm is drawn behind for a blow. His left arm carries a pelta. In the angle of the tympanum a dead Greek soldier is seen — dressed in a tunic and wearing armour — on the ground. Among all the figures in the reliefs of the sarcophagus his is the only one which shows hasty workmanship, and this only on the head and hair. On the opposite side of the pediment and at the back of the mounted Persian, another Persian is seen while covering himself with his pelta, attacking a Greek with his lance. The latter has tucked himself behind his shield waiting for a chance to run his enemy through with the sword held in his right hand. In the angle of the tympanum are a shield, and a conical Greek helmet with a crest. Among the reliefs of the sarcophagus the figures and the composition of this pediment are the least interesting.

Study of the ornamentation of the lid suggests that the artists were very familiar with the established symbolic Eastern repertoire used in sarcophagi decoration. The uppermost line of the acroterion is composed of female heads and several eagles, which have not survived but for some restored pieces of their open wings. In Syria, the eagles are known as the birds which carry the souls of the dead to heaven. The female heads, which are also seen on the two long eaves of the lid in groups of nine heads of smaller size, bring to mind the mother goddess of the Anatolian and Mesopotamian cultures worshipped since prehistoric times. Here they are thought to represent her Syrian counterpart, Atargasis, who symbolized death in winter and birth in spring. On the two ends this high acroteria finishes in a vegetal motif flanked by two "Persian griffons" placed symmetrically. They have skinny bodies of dogs, a small muzzle, thin neck and lion's paws. Between their pointed ears are two horns. Their wings bend at their back in the archaic fashion. At the four corners of the lid are open-mouthed recumbent lions, guardians of the tomb, and a common motif of Ionian art. On the long sides of the lid just below the female heads, twelve griffons of gargoyle-type are placed in imitation of gutters. Each has an animal muzzle and three horns bending towards the back.

Below the acroterion the lid is surmounted by a band of egg and tongue decoration and one of dentils. The large band of vine leaves which surrounds the lid is also related to the idea of death. These leaves were originally painted in yellow — their colour in autumn — on a wine-coloured background. After a narrow band without any ornamentation, the decoration of the lid ends with a narrow row of small palmets alternating with stylized lotus flowers and a narrow row of astragal. The two bands of decoration are the most damaged parts of the sarcophagus.

The pediment on the other side of the lid shows a skirmish or an ambush scene, which is interpreted as being related to the complicated wars which took place after the death of Alexander (323 BC) at Babylon. All the fighters are Greek soldiers, probably one group raiding another Greek camp. At the centre, a young man who is dressed in nothing but his tunic is shown fallen on his knees. On the ground his lance is indicated in colour. A soldier — armed from top to toe — has pulled the head of the young man to the back by the hair and stabs him in the shoulder. The dying man has turned as if begging for mercy, and with his two hands holds the arms of the other. However, his murderer has already turned his attention to another of the enemy. On the left, a soldier armed like the previous one is seen advancing on him. In the angle of the tympanum on this side, a Greek dressed only in a tunic is seen helping his wounded comrade, trying not to attract any attention from the others. The wounded one is armed like the soldiers at the centre of the composition and his red-coloured shield fills the corner. At the right side a Greek covering himself with his shield is seen driving his lance into his enemy who is represented already wounded and fallen on his knees. This last figure is badly damaged. His casket and shield still survive. The standing soldier is of an unusual type. He does not wear a helmet and on his head is a narrow headband. His beard is bushy and curled. His armour reflects the shape of his physique. In the background, a helmet — probably belonging to him — and a lance which must have belonged to his enemy, are shown fallen onto the ground, as well as a fleeing fighter in the angle of the tympanum and are rendered in painting.

Alexander Sarcophagus (22)

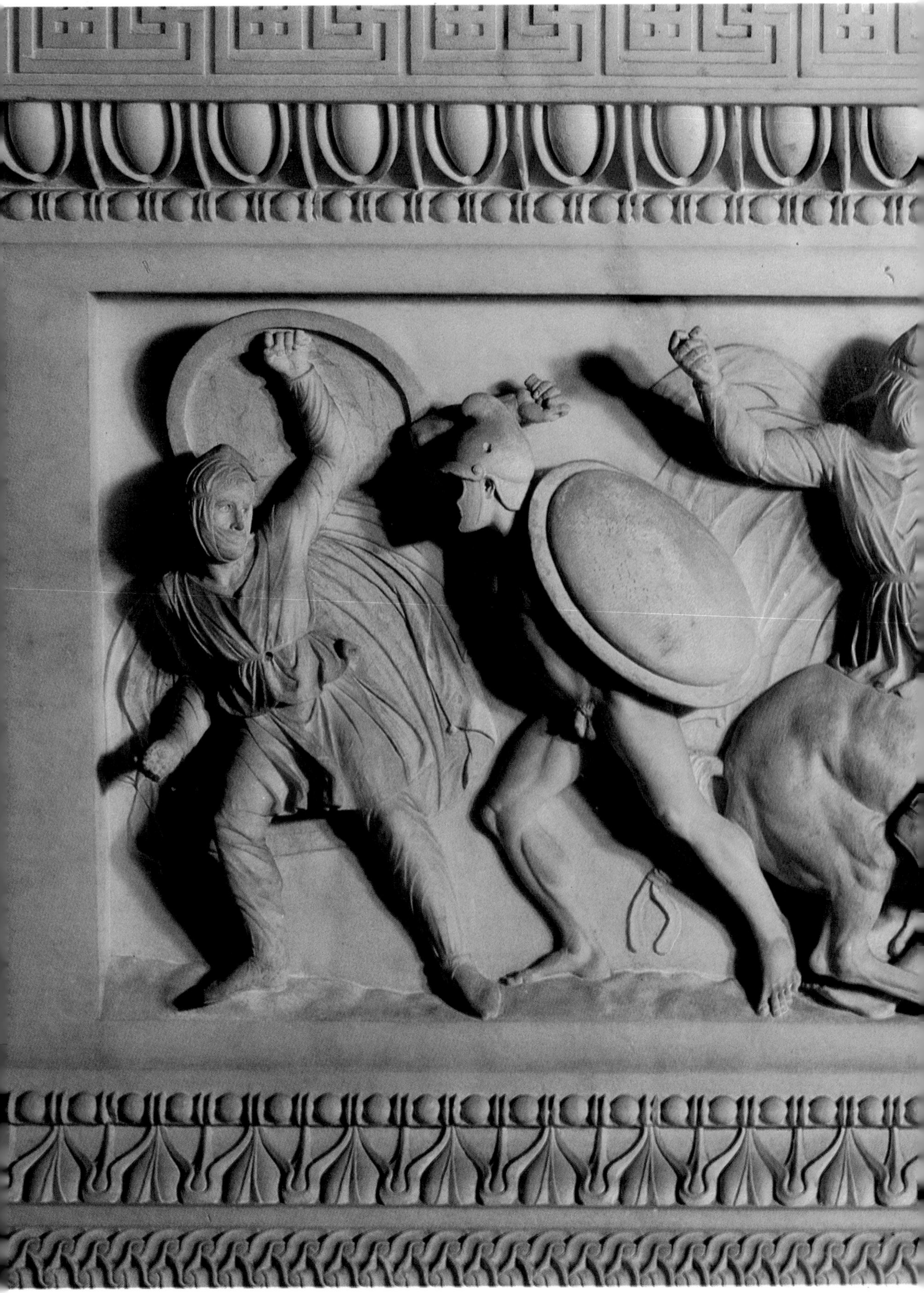

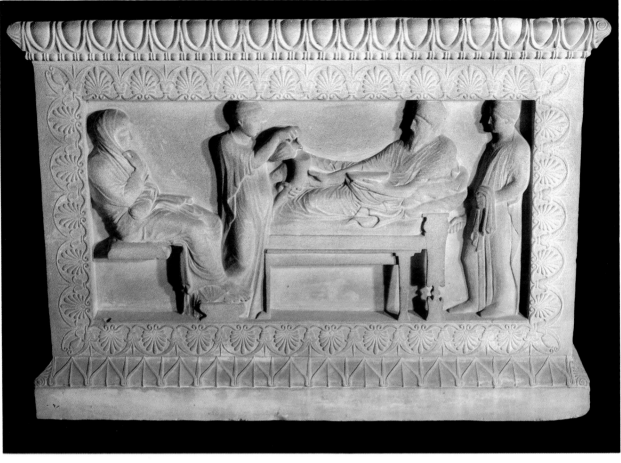

Satrap Sarcophagus (25)
Second half of 5th century BC
Sidon (Sayda)
(Inv. no 367, H. 145 cm, L. 286 cm, W. 118 cm)

Although its reliefs have suffered badly from humidity and lost their detail, this sarcophagus is regarded as an early and important example of its type. On the four sides of the casket are scenes taken from the life of an Oriental potentate. In three of these scenes the old satrap himself is included. All scenes are bordered with a large band of palmets alternating with lotus flowers. The original paint of the sarcophagus has not survived.

On one of the sort sides of the casket, the satrap is seen during a banquet in a half-reclining position on a couch. He is accompanied by his wife who is opposite him seated on a chair. Of the two male servants, the one on the left is pouring wine into a rhyton from a container in his right hand — the right arm of the satrap is extended to take the rhyton from the servant. In his other hand is a bowl. The second servant is shown standing behind his master. A napkin in his left hand; his right hand is tightly holding the handle of something — probably a fan or fly-swatter. Both servants are dressed in the Phoenician attire of the time common to their kind in Oriental countries. Under the couch of

the satrap, the silhouette of a dog — a common accessory in banquet scenes — is barely discernable.

On the other short side four young men are represented. They all carry lances and are depicted in various poses. The one on the very right seems to be listening attentively to a distant voice. These are grooms of the satrap and common figures in hunting compositions.

On one of the long sides of the casket the old satrap is shown about to start a journey. He is seated. Two of his grooms are busy preparing his quadriga. A third one is taking care of his master's horse. At the far left are placed two domestic servants. While the servant at the extreme left is a man, the second is just distinguishable as a female servant.

On the other long side the satrap is seen mounted and hunting. He is shown in the act of hurling a spear at a panther. Behind him there is a mounted groom holding the reins of his horse with both hands. Between the two a young deer already wounded, is placed. On the other side of the scene there are two more horsemen. While one of them attacks the panther the second is shown thrown from the saddle, and while being dragged by his horse — represented as if rearing up — is still trying to control it by its reins.

Next pages: **Lycian Sarcophagus** (26, 27)

LYCIAN SARCOPHAGUS

Lycian Sarcophagus (26, 27, 28, 29)
End of 5th century BC
Sidon (Sayda)
(Inv. no 369, H. 296 cm, L. 254 cm, W. 137 cm)

Although it comes from the royal necropolis at Sidon, because of its similarity in form to funeral monuments of Lycia in Anatolia, this particular sarcophagus is always referred to by this name. It is made of marble from Paros and has a lid, a casket and a marble base.

On one of the long sides of the casket a wild boar hunt is represented. Five hunters — divided into two groups of three and two — mounted on throughbred horses, are seen about to kill the boar. The horses show characteristics of their mixed Arabic and European ancestry and bring to mind those represented in the Parthenon friezes. They all have small heads with large foreheads, deep chests, broad flanks and lean bellies. These horses were the most sought-after by horse experts of antiquity. Their hooves are raised gracefully, and this stance emphasizes the sense of action. The right arms of all the hunters are raised in a uniform movement as they aim their lances at their prey. Although their faces show differences in age and the minute detail of their garments varies, they are nevertheless young men, and dressed in the typical Thracian attire which was the popular mode of fifth century Athens. Their counterparts are also to be seen in the Parthenon friezes.

On the second long side of the casket a lion hunt is depicted. Four young hunters riding on two chariots are seen trying to kill the wild animal. The horses are almost the same as those depicted on the opposite side of the casket. In placing them one behind the other in an overlapping position, a certain depth is gained. The quadrigas are seen in a three-quarter pose — a feature typical to Greek sculpture in representing chariots. The boxes in which the hunters stand, fall to the back and are ingeniously hidden from view by the rear parts of the horses and the flowing garments of the hunters. The four young men are often mistakenly interpreted as Amazons. However, neither in their garments nor in their physiognomy, except possibly for the rather feminine hairstyle of the first hunter on the left — is there anything to suggest that they were Amazons.

On one of the short sides of the casket two centaurs fighting over a deer are represented. They are seen on a rocky terrain with the front parts of their bodies against each other. While the centaur on the left is naked, a panther skin hangs from the neck of the second. The latter is about to stick the pointed end of a tree branch into the eyes of his adversary. The tympanum of the

lid on this side contains two seated sphinxes. They are represented in three-quarter poses. Their heads are turned towards the front. Their wings reach to the top of the arch of the tympanum. Their lions's bodies are modelled from those of dogs. They have female breasts and faces. The faces are drawn with a melancholic expression. They function as the guardians of the tomb.

The second short side of the casket shows the fight between the centaurs and the lapith Kaineus. According to the legend the hero, who was originally a woman, but whose sex was later changed into that of a man's by Poseidon, kills many centaurs but is unharmed owing to his charmed skin. The remaining centaurs beat him on the head with fir logs — here with an amphora and a big rock instead of logs — until they had driven him under the earth and thus killed him. In the composition Kaineus is shown already buried in the ground up to his genitals. He is naked but for a chlamys. His head which is protected by an Attic helmet is turned towards his enemies. His right hand must have held a sword. Attached to his left arm is a shield. The centaur on the left is about to bring a large amphora down on his head. The other, who carries an animal skin hanging from his neck, has raised a large piece of rock to hit him. In the tympanum of the lid on this side are placed a male and female griffon facing each other and rendered in the classical tradition of the fifth century. They are both raising three paws and standing on the remaining leg. They have eagles' heads with hissing beaks and long-horned ears. The crests which adorn their necks contain spikes. Their wings fall behind them following the curve of the arch of the lid. Their bodies — like those of the sphinxes on the opposite side — are those of a lion but modelled from a dog. Their long tails fall between their hind legs and end with a round curve. The feminine gender of the griffon on the right is emphasized by the greater number of spikes on the crest and the finer drawing of the head.

Except for the two acanthus and palmet decorations placed at the top of the tympana for acroteria, and the four lugs in the shape of recumbent lions with open mouths placed at its four corners, the lid has no other decoration. The lugs are too small to be used in transporting such a heavy lid; a secondary purpose, that of protection, is probably implied by the threatening lions.

(26)

(27)

dimensional rendering must have been intended. The sculptor has successfully combined an understanding of Peloponnesian art with the traditional Anatolian Lycian style.

Originally the surface of the sarcophagus was completely painted in various tones of red, brown and blue colours. The paint on the lid was in more vivid tones, probably to make up for the simplicity of its decoration. Neither the paint nor the metal ornamentation — the latter owing to grave robbers — have survived.

Lycian Sarcophagus (28)

Lycian Sarcophagus (29)

Although the subject matter of the scenes — except for the two short sides of the casket — are taken from Near Eastern motifs, the Lycian Sarcophagus shows no Eastern influences in the interpretation of these subjects. The sculptor of this work was probably from the Peloponnese, as he has carved the figures with stocky bodies and broad faces. The attire of the hunters and their horses show minute detail. In placing the figures one behind the other in an overlapping position a three-

GEZER CALENDAR

Gezer Calendar (30)
925 BC
Gezer (near Jerusalem)
(Inv. no 2089, H. 11 cm, W. 7.5 cm)

The Gezer Calendar is regarded as the oldest Hebrew inscription as yet known. The inscription is scratched on a tablet of limestone and its lower part is broken and lost. The oblique fracture passes a square hole thought to have been made for a peg by which it was affixed to a wall. It has seven lines of horizontal writing and the eighth line was written vertically, and only partly survives.

Although there is not much doubt about its meaning in general, there are differences of opinion as to its purpose; the final exact meaning differing from the interpretation of some signs. One of the interpretations (Père Vincent) is as follows:

"(1) Two months, late crops — Two months,
(2) Sowing — Two months, spring crops —
(3) One month, cutting flax —
(4) One month, harvest of barley —
(5) One month, all the harvest —
(6) Two months, fruit vines —
(7) One month, summer fruits
(8) Abi

The eighth line "Abi" is interpreted as the name of the person who inscribed the tablet. Some of the scholars believe that the inscription is not a calendar but a record which gives the rotation of agricultural labours, written for some unknown administrative purpose. It has also been suggested that the tablet was a kind of scrap material and some of the signs belonged to earlier writings which the scribe himself corrected.

The purpose of the tablet is not known. It is also not known whether it is the work of a peasant or a local scribe. Some hold that the roughness of the letters was probably caused by the fact that the writer probably was not used to writing on limestone. However, it is also thought that the people of an agricultural society are all so familiar with the annual rotation of labour from their childhood onwards, that the last thing they would need or think of was a catalogue or calendar of their daily work. Also nothing talismanic, magical or votive was found about it. Thus some conclude that it is the work of a peasant who wanted to display his ability to write — a harmless vanity.

In the excavations at Gezer no flax seeds were discovered and there was no indication that flax was ever grown in the area. However, it was concluded that a month may have been known as the "month of flax-harvest" even in a region where flax was not actually grown.

ירח ז | ירח אספ‎ צ | ירח (1)
רע | ירח זלקש | ירח (2)
ירח עצד פשת (3)
ירח קצר שערם (4)
(8) ירח קצר וכל‎ (5)
א ירח זמר (6)
ת ירח קץ (7)
:

(30)

(31)

Tabnit Sarcophagus (31, 32)
6th century BC
Sidon (Sayda)
(Inv. no 800, H. 106 cm, L. 233 cm, W. 108 cm)

This is the oldest of the sarcophagi which came from the royal necropolis at Sidon. Unlike the others it is made of diorite. Its lid is shaped like a head. The relief of a large necklace covers the neck and the shoulders. The Egyptian hieroglyph inscription on the chest states that it belonged to an Egyptian commander named Penephtah, and adds the customary curses to those who would interfere with it. Under this there is another inscription which belongs to Tabnit, who must be the second owner of the sarcophagus.

(32)

(33)

Anthropoid Sarcophagus of a Woman (33)
c. 460 BC
Sidon (Sayda)
(Inv. no 798, H. 75 cm, L. 226 cm, W. 93 cm)

This sarcophagus is regarded as one of the earliest examples of the group known as the "anthropoid sarcophagi". It seems that the fashion started in the fifth century and continued until the end of the 4th century. They were thought to have been produced by itinerant Greek sculptors from Egyptian models and thus they combined the Greek sculpture with exotic Oriental accessories. This particular one has handles on both sides of its shoulders and on the sides of the plinth under its feet to place it vertically. When it was discovered it carried traces of blue and red paint.

(34)

(35)

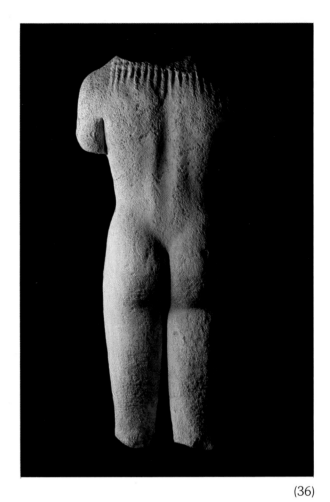

(36)

Statue of Kouros (35, 36)
Archaic, 6th century BC
Thasos
(Inv no 374, H. 135 cm)

Head of Kouros (37, 38, 39)
Archaic, 6th century BC
Samos (Sisam)
(Inv. no 1645, H. 47 cm)

His face is round and the profile is very blunt. Compared to the upper part the lower half of the face is too small. The eyes are almond-shaped and slightly turned towards the outer side. The eyeballs are very flat. The eyebrow arches high. The nose is long with the mouth placed very close to it. The lips are closed and straight. The grooves at the corners give the impression that he is smiling. The jaw is bony and separated from the lower lip by another deep depression. The cheeks are fleshy, the cheekbones projecting. The ears are too big — but are set with almost exact precision on the sides of the head. His hair is done very carefully. The roots of the hair are depicted as a narrow vertical zone with all the single hairs pressed together above the forehead. Beyond this line the hair is plaited and falls to the neck. This is the head of a Greek youth or "kouros" which constitute a homogen group and represent certain characters of South Ionian Archaic art. Similar heads or statues are often discovered in Samos, Rhodes or Cos.

Colossal Statue of Bes (40)
Roman, 1st—3rd century AD
Amathus (Cyprus)
(Inv. no 3317, H. 350 cm, W. 175 cm)

Bes — originally a semi-god of ancient Egypt — was very popular in the Cypriot pantheon of gods and often confused with Herakles. In the statue he is shown holding a headless lioness by its hind legs. The big hole at the god's loins was probably the seat of a colossal phallus. It has been politely claimed that it might have served as a fountain.

(37)

(38)

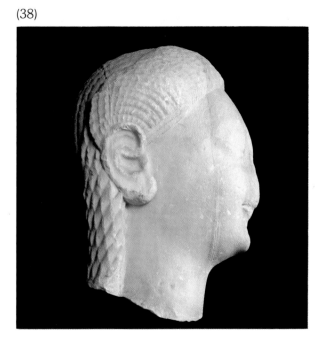

(39)

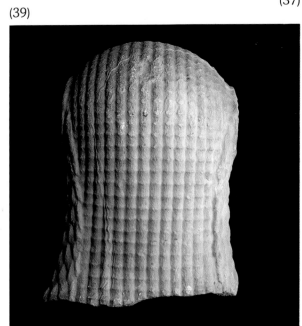

(40)

Pyramidal Funeral Stele (41)
Late Archaic, second quarter of 5th century BC
Sinope (Sinop)
(Inv. no 3868, H. 66 cm)

Frieze from the Temple of Athena (42)
Archaic, c. 530 BC
Assos (Behramkale)
(Inv. no 245, 247—249; architrave frieze inv. no 245, H. 81 cm,
L. 260 cm)

In the metope of the frieze two combatants — one carrying a heavy sword — and a man chasing a younger one, are separated by a triglyph. In the architrave a group of four centaurs are depicted scared of something and running away. The temple of Athena of Assos is known as the only Doric temple in Anatolia of the Archaic period. The friezes are of basalt, a most durable material and rarely used in architecture.

(41)

(42)

47

(43)

(44)

(45)

Stele of Proxeni Dedicated to a Citizen of Panticape (43, 44)
4th century BC
Cyzicus (Erdek)
(Inv. no 35, H. 52.5 cm, W. 47.5 cm)

At the centre of the stele Pan is shown in a concave medallion. One long pointed ear is visible among his long locks of hair drawn to the back. He has a drooping moustache and pointed beard. Around his neck an animal skin — often worn by satyrs in Classic art — is seen. The stele is decorated with a band of egg and tongue and a thinner band of astragal. It was used as a second time for another dedication in the Roman period. These later users also copied the band of decoration on the original side but unskilfully.

Greco-Persian Funeral Stele (45)
5th century BC
Daskylaion (Aksakal, Manyas)
(Inv. no 5763, H. 221 cm, W. 62 cm)

This stele is regarded as one of the finest examples of its kind. It obviously belonged to a transporter of goods. It combines tha characteristics of both Persian and Greek sculptures. The cart with its many-spoked wheels, the horses with their tails bound tightly in the middle, the crown worn by the seated woman and the high boots worn by men, are all features of Persian art while the form of the stele, the tripod and the vessel on top and the wife and her husband intimately sitting together are all typical of Greek art.

(47)

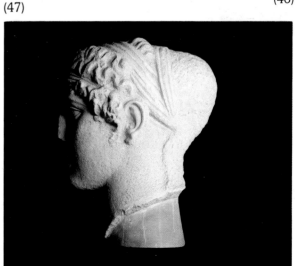

(46)

Colossal Head of a Goddess (46, 47)
Roman, 2nd century AD
Smyrna (Izmir)
(Inv. no 358, H. 90 cm)

The goddess has an oval and fleshy face. The lips are strong and with grooves. On the middle part of the upper lip a lump — almost as if swollen — is seen. Her lower lip is larger. Her eyes are carefully worked with deep cuts. The front part of the hair is arranged in large curls. A headband is bound over her hair twice horizontally and then once more vertically. At the back the hair falls below the neck in softer curls. This is one of the type known under the name of "Sappho" or more commonly "Aphrodite".

Herm of Hermes Propylaios (48)
Roman, 2nd century AD
Pergamum
(Inv. no 1433, H. 119.5 cm)

The arms of the statue have not survived. The details of Hermes' head are sculpted with almost geometric precision. His hairstyle is arranged in three bands of hair in imitation of a diadem. His eyes and mouth are drawn very horizontal, and his nose, the ends of his moustache and his beard are completely vertical. On both sides of his head two thick locks of hair fall from his headdress and reach to his chest. The inscription informs us that it is a statue of Hermes by Alkamenes and offered by the people of Pergamum. The original statue must have been sculpted by the fifth century BC Greek sculptor Alkamenes, and our sculptor, when he copied it, must have copied the inscription on the original statue as well. At the lowest part of the statue the genitals of the god are exposed.

Statue of Artemis (49)
Roman, 2nd—3rd century AD
Lesbos (Midilli)
(Inv. no 121, H. 107 cm)

The goddess is seen standing on her lef leg. Her right foot is crossed over the other. Her right arm is resting on a pillar. The other arm is on her hip with the palm of the hand facing outward. Her hair is divided into two sections and covers part of her ears. Two short forelocks are seen close to her ears. Originally her head carried a diadem. Her arms are decorated with snake-shaped bracelets. Her high boots leave her toes bare. The statue is regarded as being not a good specimen of its kind. Her clothes are rather stiff, especially over the hips. Her left hand is unusually long and the arms are attached to the body in an unlikely manner.

Funeral Stele of Telemachos (50)
4th century BC
Athens
(Inv. no 577, H. 93 cm, W. 34 cm)

Caryatid (51, 52)
Roman, 1st century AD
Tralles (Aydın)
(Inv. no 1189, H. 186 cm)

A young woman is shown standing with her weight almost equally balanced on her two legs. Both of her feet touch the ground completely. Her left arm is raised above her head as if she would carry the architrave which would have been placed on her cylindrical headdress (polos). Although the statue is that of a caryatid it is not necessarily thought that it was designed as an architectural element of a building. Her right arm hangs at her side and holds her himation. She is dressed in a chiton which gives the impression of being made of a special material, almost metallic. Her himation is of simple cut in two pieces of different length. Her bosom is well-shaped. Her breasts are pointed and separated from each other distinctively. Her hair is arranged meticulously and tied by a headband at the back. Three long locks fall on her chest on both sides of the head in metallic curves ending with a lock in the shape of a question mark. Her head is small and round. Her eyes long and narrow. Her nose has large nostrils. Her lips are slightly curved. Her jaw is large, strong and separated from the lower lip by a depression. The sculptor has neglected her ears though. Her feet are shod in sandals.

This stele is regarded as a good specimen of its kind. The figure of a young boy whose name is carved above his head is placed between two pillars without capitals. The triangular pediment of the niche is decorated with three massive acroterion. On the boy's head a band is seen. His long and curly hair falls onto his ears. His tunic is wrapped around his left forearm. His feet are shod in sandals of thin leather. In his left hand are a stirigil and a vessel for oil. With his other hand he seems to be holding a small bird. The attention of the dog at his feet is turned towards the bird.

52)

51)

STATUES OF MILETUS

The statues of Miletus which are on display in the museum were discovered during the excavations carried out by the Berlin Museum at the beginning of the present century. Those included in this publication all come from the Baths of Faustina — after the second empress of that name — which were built in the second century AD and underwent several modifications in the following century. These statues are thought to have been copied from a group of statues which were produced by the famous sculptor Philiscus of Rhodes in the late 3rd century BC.

Statue of Apollo (53, 54)
Roman, 2nd century AD
Miletus
(Inv. no 2000, H. 177 cm)

Apollo is rendered here as a muscular young man. He has a divine and peaceful expression on his face and his body is graceful and well-proportioned. The rather feminine sensuality portrayed is probably caused by his over-emphasized hips. The short legs are an inexcusable fault on the part of the sculptor who copied the statue from its Hellenistic original. The god stands on his right leg with his body swaying to the opposite side — towards the pillar. At the top of this pillar is placed an ornamented lyre. His fingers must originally have been touching the strings of the instrument. His right arm is raised with his forearm lightly resting on his head, and his hand is holding the plectrum of the lyre as if playing on the strings before beginning the melody. This form of rendering of the god was known as Apollo "citharados" or "playing the lyre". His robe falls below his waist leaving his genitals exposed. His sandals are the most attractive part of his attire. The buckle of his left sandal, his shoulder-belt and his face still bear traces of reddish-brown paint. Traces of reddish-brown and blue paint can be distinguished on the lyre as well.

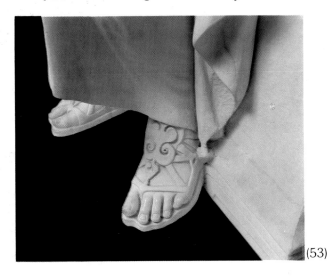

(53)

Statue of Terpsichore (55)
Roman, 2nd century AD
Miletus
(Inv. no 2007, H. 139 cm)

Terpsichore, the mother of sirens, is depicted in a soft dancing movement with her body slightly swaying to her right side. She is dressed in a tunic and a cloak. Her right foot is bare and steps on an irregular plinth. The fragments of the fingers of her right hand have survived holding a piece of her drapery.

Statue of a Muse (56)
Roman, 2nd century AD
Miletus
(Inv. no 1994, H. 170 cm)

This muse is represented with her weight on her right leg. Her left shoulder is slightly higher than the other. Her head is leisurely turned to her right and inclined towards her right shoulder. A slight pathos is given to the expression on her face. The mouth is shown almost open. Large eyebrows make complete arches above round eyes. Her hairstyle is in harmony with the lines of her face. Above the forehead the hair is separated into two and is arranged on both sides in irregular curls. Close to her ears on each side two deep furrows are placed. She has a rather complicated drapery of three pieces which are secured on her shoulders by small buttons or buckles. The long tunic falls in a deep pleat between her legs — a very clever artistic touch.

Statue of Melpomene (57)
Roman, 2nd century AD
Miletus
(Inv. no 1993, H. 155 cm)

This statue of the muse is seen standing with her weight on her left side. She is dressed in two pieces of cloth which surround the body baring only the neck and arms. Her right arm which is stretched out and raised above her shoulder is supported by a clumsy length of marble which is placed between her right side and her right elbow. Her other arm hangs down on her other side. In this hand is held a mask of Herakles — the tragic hero par excellence — identified by the pelt of the lion.

Statue of a Muse with a Double-flute (58)
Roman, 2nd century AD
Miletus
(Inv. no 1999, H. 147 cm)

Statue of a Muse with a Lyre (59)
Roman, 2nd century AD
Miletus
(Inv. no 2002, H. 161 cm)

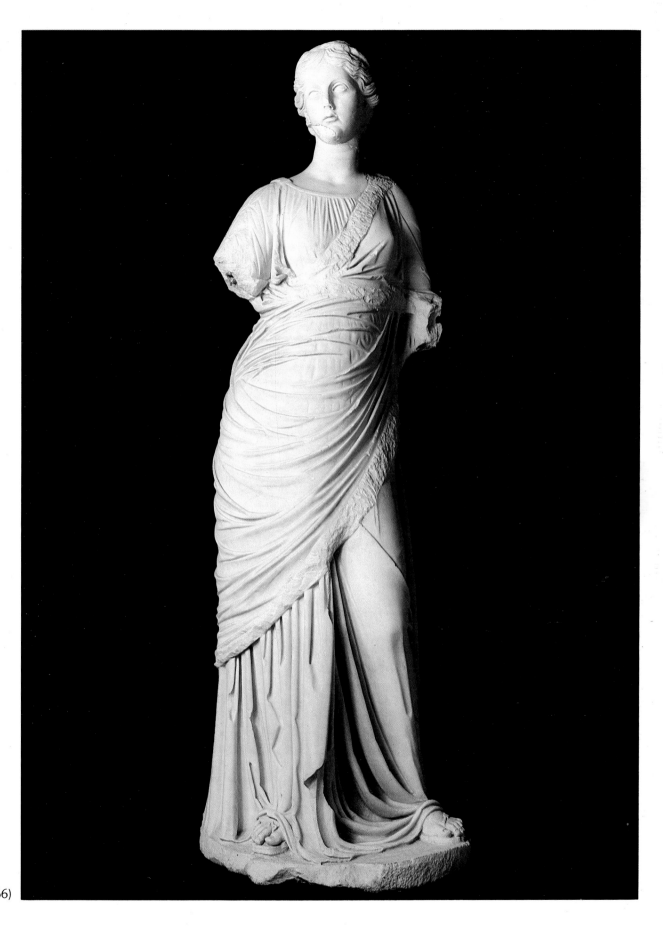

6)

ALEXANDER THE GREAT

Statue of Alexander the Great (62)
Hellenistic, 2nd century BC
Magnesia-ad-Siplyum (Manisa)
(Inv. no 709, H. 190 cm)

This statue was hewn from white marble of very fine quality. The existence of a row of indentation around the head indicates that it was once crowned with a metal laurel wreath. The right arm and hand of the statue have not survived. Originally this hand held a bronze spear. The hilt of the sword in the left hand still survives.

What distinguishes this from similar statues of Alexander exhibited in various museums of the world is that, it was discovered accompanied by an inscription which reads, "Menas of Pergamon, son of Aias, made [it]" thus indicating its origin. The rendering of the upper part of the torso naked, the disposition of the body, and the meditative expression with slightly open lips are characteristics of portrayals of gods, especially Apollo, in the Hellenistic era.

HEAD OF ALEXANDER THE GREAT

Head of Alexander the Great (61)
Hellenistic, first half of 2nd century BC
Pergamum
(Inv. no 1138, H. 42 cm)

Originally the statue to which this head was attached, stood in Pergamum overlooking the second century lower agora of the city. (It has recently been suggested by some archaeologists that the head was originally part of the decoration of the "Altar of Zeus".) The drooping of the head onto the shoulder and its very slight backward inclination, the great mane of hair rising from the middle of the forehead like that of a lion's mane, and its falling on both sides in uneven locks, the round eyes with heavy lids and thick eyebrows, and the slightly open mouth which does not quite reveal the teeth, are all characteristic of sculptures of Alexander. The type dates back to the fourth century BC to the portrayal of Alexander by the fourth century BC sculptor Lysippus. Here, the over-all impression is of a sensitive face with soft lines and with a touching melancholy. The deeply furrowed forehead brings to mind the enormous problems he had already encountered although so young, and with regard to its realistic rendering, is typical of the Pergamane art of sculpture during the reign of king Eumenes II (195—59 BC). The "Dying Gaul" at the Capitoline Museum in Rome and the heads in the friezes of the "Altar of Zeus" in the Berlin Museum, are among other examples of the Pergamane school of sculpture in which the same style is observed.

EPHEBE

Statue of an Ephebe (60)
Late 1st century BC—early 1st century AD
Tralles (Aydın)
(Inv. no 1191, H. 148 cm)

Originally, this statue was probably a part of the decoration of a gymnasium. Archaeologists do not agree as to its exact date. It shows a very young — assumed to be around twelve years old — athlete, leaning against a pillar which was once decorated with a bust or relief, while he recovers from his strenuous exertions. He must have just finished his exercise because his body is wrapped around in a tunic to prevent his catching cold. Over this he wears a thick mantle which brings to mind the type commonly used by shepherds in eastern countries. He has muscular legs and his feet are shod in leather sandals.

The flowing lines of his relaxed body are ingeniously hidden by his garments, and thus the attention of the onlooker is drawn to his small round head which is depicted tilted slightly forward. The swollen ears indicate that the youth is also a wrestler. The large eyes, and the childish charming face with its air of mystery are often encountered among the Mediterranean peoples. This head is unequalled by any other head of antiquity so far discovered.

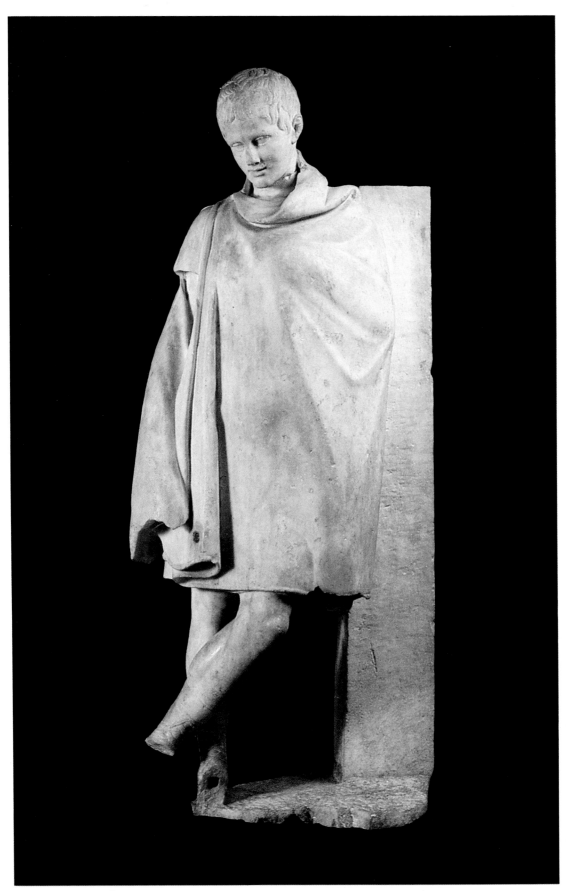

1)

6

Statue of Marsyas (63, 64)
Hellenistic, second half of 3rd century BC
Tarsos (Tarsus)
(Inv. no 400, H. 130 cm)

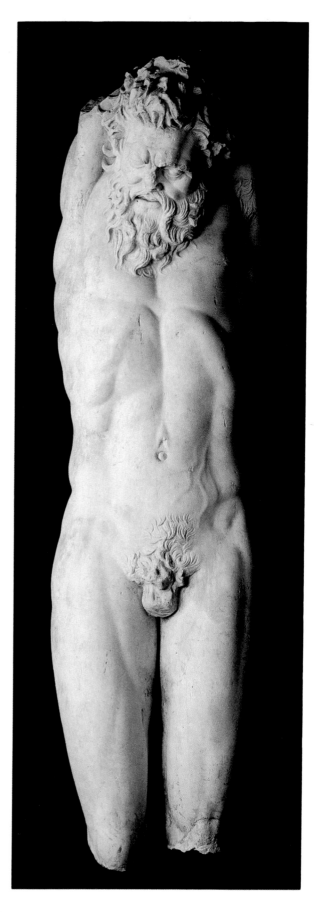

Marsyas is depicted suspended from a tree by his arms. Although he was often sculpted as an isolated statue, this particular statue was originally placed at the centre of a group with a seated Apollo on his left and a Scythian slave sharpening a knife to flay him on his right. In order to display the tortured body of Marsyas better, the sculptor has preferred to depict Marsyas as a rather skinny satyr. The tightened muscles of the body are clearly noticed in the suspended body. His head has fallen on his chest and has turned a little to his right. His mouth is slightly open as if a groan will escape from his lips. The deformed eyebrows almost join each other above his hollow eyes. His nose is short. Above a broad forehead his hair is raised in disorder. Although it is not original, this statue is one of the best of its kind, and its detail brings to mind the characteristics of the giants' reliefs of the "Altar of Zeus", and thus the sculpture of the Pergamene school during the time of Eumenes II.

According to the legend, when the peasants heard the notes of the flute of Marsyas they cried out that Apollo himself could not have made better music with his lyre, and Marsyas was foolish enough not to contradict them. When the music contest afterwards with Apollo proved an equal one, Apollo said "I challenge you to do with your instrument as much as I can do with mine. Turn it upside down, and both play and sing at the same time". Thus Marsyas failed to meet the challenge, and Apollo reversed the lyre and sang and played it and won the contest.

(65)

Head of a Hero or Heroine (65)
Hellenistic, 2nd century BC
Cos (İstanköy)
(Inv. no 1524, H. 31.5 cm)

The head originally carried a big Corinthian helmet which covered the ears as well. Only a small part of this helmet survives on the neck. Some of the hair falls below the ears in big locks. The lines of the face are cold and the work lacks individuality. The large nose destroys the rather sentimental over-all impression. It is a hasty work, probably inspired by a Pergamene original of a statue of the idealized Alexander.

Statue of Hermaphrodite (67)
Hellenistic, 3rd century BC
Pergamum
(Inv. no 363, H. 186.5 cm)

This statue is shown standing with its weight on the right leg and the body swaying in the opposite direction. Its left leg does not touch the ground but for the toes. The left arm rests on a tree trunk. The right arm must have been hanging down, for traces have survived at the edge of the cloth on the hip. Its sandals are decorated with winged sphinxes. Its only garment is a cloak which leaves the torso completely naked in the front. The sex of Hermaphrodite is rendered very discreetly. The lower parts of the body, the hips and modestly drawn genitals belong to a young man. The navel, well-shaped breasts with enlarged nipples, the head and especially the hairstyle are all feminine. The head carries a headband. Two long locks fall on the shoulders and two small locks are left close to the ears. The long narrow eyes have a distant look. The idea of melancholy — common to all depictions of Hermaphrodite — is strengthened by the drawing of the mouth. The statue is regarded as a very good copy of the original.

(66)

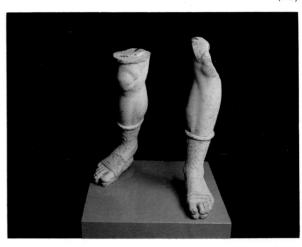

Legs of a Statue (66)
Late 3rd—early 2nd century BC
Cyme (Namurt Harbour)
(Inv. no 389—390, H. 64 and 68 cm)

The statue to which these legs were attached obviously stood with the weight on the left leg. The right one is drawn behind and the sole of the foot does not touch the ground completely. The statue was probably dressed in armour over a short tunic. A piece of this tunic has survived above the right knee. The feet are shod in button-up sandals which are richly decorated by a pattern of foliage design. Only the toes are left bare. These legs give the impression that the statue was of a Hellenic nobleman. The legs did not stand on a marble plinth. They must have been fixed on a kind of wooden base by the sole of the feet like the bronze statues. This was a risky and thus rare method used on marble statues.

7

(68)

Statue of a Nymph (68, 69, 70)
Late Hellenistic or early Roman Imperial, 1st century
BC—early 1st century AD
Tralles (Aydın)
(Inv. no 1190, H. 166 cm)

The large bust and hips of this statue, confirm the fashion of this period for more voluptuous females to be depicted in sculpture. The statue must have originally been a part of a fountain decoration, because calcerous deposits on the drapery and left foot have survived to the present day.

(69)

Statue of Cornelia Antonia (71)

Roman, 2nd century AD
Antioch of Pisidia (Yalvaç)
(Inv. no 2645, H. 203 cm)

(71)

The statue is identified by an inscription on its base. It is clothed in a long voluminuous robe which covers the entire body and falls onto the plinth. Although the pose of the body and the disposition of the hands is classic, in the eyes, nose and mouth, a successful attempt towards achieving individual characterization may be observed.

(70)

(72)

Column Capital with Animal Figures (72)
Byzantine, 6th century AD
Istanbul, Tophane
(Inv. no 5452, H. 55 cm, W. 70—78 cm)

River God (74)
Roman, 2nd century AD
Ephesus
(Inv. no 4281, H. 127 cm, L. 217 cm)

Relief of Gigantomachy (73)
Roman, 2nd century AD
Aphrodisias
(Inv. no 1613A, H. 119 cm, L. 210 cm)

On the left side of the relief next to a tree the goddess Athena is seen attacking two giants. She is dressed in two pieces of drapery which reach to the ground. Her chest is covered by a small piece of armour. She wears an arched helmet with a big plume of two pieces. Attached to her left arm she carries a round shield whose concave side is visible. In her right hand which was drawn behind and above her shoulder she must have had a lance. The two gians who have legs of serpents are seen trying to run away from the goddess. The one seen close to the tree at the centre of the composition raises his weaponless right arm towards Athena as if to protect himself from the coming blow. He is mortally wounded and his head has fallen onto his left shoulder. His disorderly long hair is high on his forehead. He has a drooping moustache, beard, and some whiskers on his cheeks. Like his companion he carries a lion's pelt on his left arm. In this hand there must have been a heavy club in the shape of a boulder because the hole to which it was attached still survives. The second giant is shown from the back. He is older than his friend. While using a lion's pelt as a shield, his right arm is raised and he seems to be throwing a piece of rock at the goddess.

(73)

(74)

(75)

Sleeping Eros (75)
Roman, 1st century AD
Tralles (Aydın)
(Inv. no 250, L. 58 cm)

The small god is given the trophy of Herakles. He is seen asleep on the ground on Herakles' lion pelt. His wings are open under his body. His legs are crossed, left one over the right. His left arm supports his head. His right arm is stretched across his chest and with his hand he holds the club of Herakles. His curly hair is hidden by the lion's mouth and Amon's ram horn.

Sarıgüzel Sarcophagus (76)
Byzantine, c. 400 AD
Istanbul, (Fatih, Sarıgüzel)
(Inv. no 4508, H. 55 cm, L. 150 cm)

This sarcophagus probably belonged to a nobleman. On each of its long sides, a pair of angels in flight holding between them a circular monogram are represented. On the short sides are placed a pair of bearded apostles flanking a cross.

(76)

(77)

(78)

(79)

Head of Artemis (77)
Hellenistic, 3rd—2nd century BC
Cyme (Namurt Harbour)
(Inv. no 386, H. 39 cm)

The head is turned slightly towards the left shoulder. The face is naturally oval. It has a small and rather nice mouth almost smiling. The eyes originally were painted. The hair is done in two parts and covers half of the ears. It is a hasty but not unsuccessful work. The ears originally had holes for earrings. On the head there must have been a metal stephane. The hole by which it was attached to the head is still visible. The head is regarded as a very good copy of the original.

Head of Emperor Arcadius (?) (78)
Late Roman, end of 4th century AD
Istanbul, Beyazıt
(Inv. no 5028, H. 33 cm)

Bust of Emperor Marcus Aurelius (79)
Roman, second half of 2nd century AD
Bilecik, Bozhöyük (Kandilli Village)
(Inv. no 5129, H. 92 cm)

Head of Emperor Lucius Verus (80)
Roman, second half of 2nd century AD
Antioch of Pisidia (Yalvaç)
(Inv. no 2646, H. 33 cm)

Baluster (81)
Byzantine, Mid-5th—early 6th century AD
Izmit, Değirmendere
(Inv. no 4477, H. 118 cm, W. 25 cm)

(81)

(80)

Column Drum (82)
Byzantine, 5th—6th century AD
Istanbul
(Inv. no 901, H. 75 cm, diam. c. 62.5 cm)

This is the upper drum of a column. At the top it
has a projecting band decorated with stylized branches.
Below this is a rather crowded low relief which surround
the drum completely. In this vegetal background human
figures and animals are distributed. At the central part
a young shepherd is shown standing on a vine branch
and holding a long stick in the left hand and a dog by
a thick rope in the other. On his right an older villager
is represented ploughing. Between the two figures is a
goat, and on the left side of the young shepherd, an
ox is seen.

Deep Bowl (84)
Byzantine, end of 13th century AD
Istanbul (Hagia Eirene)
(Inv. no 71.77, H. 8.2 cm, diam. 15 cm)

This bowl of glazed pottery has a partridge with leaf motifs as decoration.

(83)

Perfume Bottle (Alabastron) (83)
Phrygian, end of 7th—beginning of 6th century BC
Gordium, Tumulus II
(Inv. no 1360, H. 44 cm, W. 10 cm)

Figurine of Two Women Dancing (86)
Hellenistic, 3rd—1st century BC
Çanakkale, Intepe
(Inv. no 692, H. 27 cm)

Fragment of Pyxis (85)
Byzantine, 6th century AD
Istanbul
(Inv. no 8054, H. 7.8 cm)

Worked in ivory, this shows three magicians, the Virgin, and an angel holding the world in his hand.

(85)

(86)

Hydria with Relief Scene (87)
Late Classic, Mid-4th century BC
Lampsakos (Lapseki)
(Inv. no 2922, H. 48 cm)

Figure of Aphrodite Holding a Mirror (89)
Hellenistic, Mid-2nd century BC
Myrina
(Inv. no 390, H. 25 cm)

(88)

(89)

Icon of Saint Eudokia (88)
Byzantine, 11th century AD
Istanbul (Fenari Isa Cami — former Monastery of
Constantine Lips)
(Inv. no 4309, H. 66 cm, W. 28 cm)

Saint Eudokia is shown wearing a robe and crown
inlaid with precious stones. Her hands are raised in
prayer. Her name is inscribed on both sides of her
nimbed head.

(91)

Reliquary Cross (92)
Byzantine, 6th—7th centuries AD
Gönen
(Inv. no 71.247, H. 9.3 cm)

(90)

Gold Earring (90)
Middle Byzantine, 9th—beginning of 13th century AD
Provenance unknown
(Inv. no 77.131, H. 4.3 cm, W. 3 cm)

Gold Pendant Headgear (91)
Early Bronze Age, second half of 3rd millenium BC
Troy II or III (?), Treasure C (?)
(Inv. no 676A—676B, L. 25 cm)

Gold medallion (93)
Byzantine, 6th century AD
Adana
(Inv. no 82a, diam. 8.2 cm)

(93)

(92)

Pitcher with Beak Spout (94)
Phrygian, middle of 8th—beginning of 7th century BC
Gordium, Tumulus III
(Inv. no 3041, H. 16 cm, diam. (body) 14 cm)

Lamp with Stand (95)
Early Byzantine, 4th—6th century AD
Provenance unknown
(Inv. no 6113, H. 34 cm)

(94)

Small Flask in the Shape of a Woman's Bust (96)
Orientalizing, Late 7th century BC
Pitane (Çandarlı)
(Inv. no 9965, H. 10 cm)

(96)

(95)

Çinili Köşk. Exterior (97)

ÇINILI KÖŞK

Blue-and-White Ceramic Mosque Lamp (98)
First quarter of 16th century
Iznik
(Inv. no 41/2, H. 27.6 cm, diam. 18.2 cm)

Çinili Köşk, or the "Tiled Pavilion" is the smallest museum of the complex. Until larger premises were added to it towards the end of the 19th century, this two-storey building housed miscellaneous antiquities.

It is known as the oldest secular building in Istanbul, and was built in 1472 during the time of Mehmet II, the Conqueror. Records and miniature paintings show that the pavilion was used by the sultan and palace dignitaries to watch sports activities such as wrestling or "jirid", a kind of polo game popular among the Turks.

In design and decoration the building is inspired by Seljuk art. Above its door, covering the three faces of the entrance alcove in a large band, there is a beautiful inscription in underglazed technique; white letters on a dark blue background and each letter with a yellow subordinate. This inscription confirms the date of construction. The rest of this recessed entrance is also covered with tiles, mostly in turquoise and dark blue colours which include highly stylized cufic calligraphy. At one time all the rooms of this small pavilion were

decorated with triangular and hexagonal tiles in turquoise and dark blue, similar to those in the Yeşil Cami or the "Green Mosque" at Bursa. Some of the tiles of Çinili Köşk have survived to the present intact, and the building at present, appropriately, is used as a museum of Turkish tiles and ceramics.

However, until the foundation of the Turkish Republic, foreign wares were more highly valued than local products, and thus a large number of the finest Turkish pottery found its way into foreign collections and museums. At present, in addition to some very fine examples of the pottery of Iznik and Kütahya, the rooms of the museum house beautiful mosque lamps, plates, bowls, wall panels from different mosques and a fountain and 19th century Çanakkale pottery. Among the important works of art is the mihrap of Ibrahim Bey Cami (1432) from Karaman.

(98)

(99)

(100)

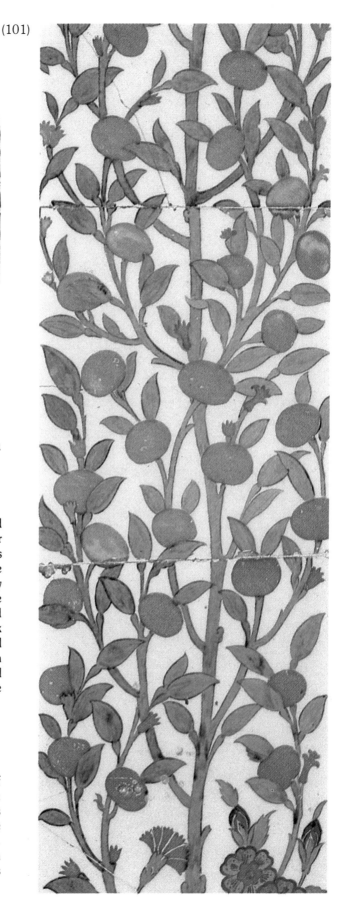

(101)

Blue and Turquoise Hexagonal Tile (100)

c. 1530—40

Iznik

(Inv. no 41/517, diam. 21.7 cm)

Mosque Lamp from Sokullu Mehmet Paşa Cami (99)

c. 1572

Iznik

(Inv. no 41/16, H. 47.5 cm, diam. 29 cm)

The lamp is painted underglaze in black, brushed cobalt, bole-red and turquoise. Its neck bears a prayer in white "sülüs" on a blue ground. Between the letters blossoms and leaves are scattered. The lettering is done by a very skilful calligrapher. The body is separately produced. Between the handles there are three hemispherical bosses which show an eight-petalled flower in red at the centre of each, surrounded by black "rumis". Originally these bosses were gilded. A scroll with three large and three smaller blossoms and much smaller blossoms of a different shape and tendrils fill remainder of the lamp surface. It is a very fine piece suitable as a gift for the inauguration of a mosque.

Polychrome Tile Panel (101)

Second half of 16th century

Iznik

(Inv. no 41/1412, H. 94 cm, W. 28.5 cm)

The panel is composed of three large squares of underglazed-painted tiles. The squares are larger than the usual size produced in Iznik kilns. The panel is thought to have been made after an order. At the bottom a carnation and another blue blossom are seen. The rest of the panel is dominated by a green tree with the same colour branches and leaves bearing red flowers and fruits.

(102)

(103)

Gate Lion (103)
Late Hittite, 832—810 BC
Zinjirli (Sam'al)
(Inv. no 7701, H. 200 cm, L. 297 cm)

Statue of a Deified King (102)
End of 3rd—beginning of 2nd millenium BC
Babylon
(Inv. no 7813, H. 165 cm)

This statue was dedicated to a temple by Pusur-Ishtar, Governor of Mari. It was found in the 6th century "Palace Museum" at Babylon, which contained antiquities collected by King Nebuchadrezzar of the Late Babylonian period and his ancestors. Its head is moulded from the original in the Berlin Museum (East Germany).

Inscribed Gate Lion (104)
Late Hittite, *c.* 800 BC
Maraş
(Inv. no 7698, H. 63 cm)

This is a guardian statue made in basalt. The animal figure itself is not very detailed, owing to the hieroglyph inscription covering the entire body. The forequarters and head of the lion are sculpted in the round; the rest of the body is in relief.

MUSEUM OF THE ANCIENT ORIENT

This is the first of the three buildings in the museum complex to greet the visitor; its entrance is protected by two beautiful basalt lions of the Hittite period. The building was constructed in 1883 and originally served as the Academy of Fine arts. After it was added to the museum complex in 1917, it was used for the display of various kinds of collections from the Anatolian, Egyptian and Mesopotamian civilizations.

Although not large in number the objects on display are very important specimens of the cultures to which they belong. Among the Anatolian civilizations represented in the museum the Hittite and the Urartu are the most important. The objects which belonged to Mesopotamia, Egypt, and the pre-Islamic culture of the Arabic peninsula, are those which came from the excavations carried out in the second half of the nineteenth century just before these lands broke away from the Ottoman Empire. They were collected and sent to the museum by conscientious governors of various provinces in these lands.

The museum was closed in 1963, and after a long period of extensive restorations, re-opened to the public in 1974. It is the most modern section of the museum complex, and despite its small size it is one of the most important of its kind in the world.

(104)

(10.

Lion Relief (105)
Neo-Babylonian, early 6th century BC
Babylon
(Inv. no 88.142, H. 105 cm, L. 209 cm)

Babylon is known as the last Mesopotamian monarchy, in which the three thousand year self-rule in Mesopotamia came to an end. Nebuchadrezzar (604—562 BC) was the last of its hero-kings. During his rule the city saw its last glorious days. In the Old Testament texts (the Book of Daniel) the king is known as "Nebuchadnezzar" who sacked Jerusalem and deported thousands of Jews to Babylonia. During his time Babylon covered some 500 acres, with a population of approximately one hundred thousand people.

The streets of Nebuchadrezzar's city were laid parallel to the Euphrates, which divided the city into two, in a modern manner. Eight gates provided access. However — excluding the renowned "Hanging Gardens" — the hallmark of his architectural achievements was the "Ishtar Gate" by which the main highway entered the city and took the name of "Procession Street". This double gate and its walls adjoining Procession Street had their outer faces covered with various designs of coloured glazed brickwork in blue, yellow and black. Repeated at regular

(106)

Bull Relief (106)
Neo-Babylonian, early 6th century BC
Babylon
(Inv. no 88.147, H. 145 cm, L. 165 cm)

intervals there were figures of all sorts of beasts and dragons, such as lions, bulls and "sirrush" dragon. During the New Year's Festival the statues of the gods were carried along this street. Later in his reign Nebuchadrezzar built a second palace close to this gate. Excavations indicated that this building was used as a museum in which works of art dating back to the end of the third millenium were collected, and it is thought that this interest in antiquities was cultivated by more than one king of the Neo-Babylonian dynasty. Some of the important antiquities in this museum come from this building.

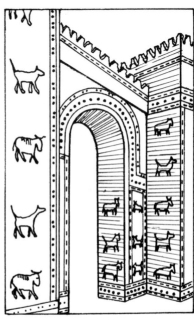

The Ishtar Gate, as reconstructed in the Staacliche Museum, East Berlin

(107)

Cuneiform Tablet (107)
1900 BC
Kültepe, Kanesh
(Inv. no Ka. 135, 6.8 × 5.5 × 2 cm)

The baked clay cuneiform tablet is a letter addressed by one merchant to another concerning the latter's debts to him. In the sections near the upper and lower edges there are finger nail marks pressed there as a personal seal.

The Akkadian cuneiform (from Latin *cuneus* — wedge, and *forma* — form) was the international script of the main powers, the Hittites, the Mitanni and Egypt in the second millenium BC, and was applied on moist clay held in the left hand with a reed stylus. It reads from left to right and top to bottom. However, when the front face was finished, it did not turn like a page of a book, but on its horizontal axis. Thus the writing on the back of a tablet was always upside down.

Beak-spouted Pitcher (108)
Old Hittite, 16th century BC
Tokat (not an excavation find)
(Inv. no 12890, H. 30 cm)

The spouted pitchers constitute a very distinct group of Hittite pottery. This particular one must have been used for ritual purposes. The body was made on a potter's wheel in the shape of a dagger. The ring-shaped ornaments are interpreted as holy symbols preventing profane use. Its handle is a long cylindrical neck resembling the beak of a bird of prey.

(108)

(109)

Gate Orthostat Showing a Royal Chariot and Guards (109)

Late Assyrian, second half of 8th century BC
Hadatu (Aslantaş)
(Inv. no 1946—1947, H. 100 cm, L. 186 cm)

Ceremonial Vessel (110)

Early Bronze Age, end of 3rd millenium BC
Troy III, IV (?)
(Inv. no 1993 (Arch. Mus.), H. 14.5 cm, diam. 12.4 cm)

The vessel is handmade and assumed to represent the mother goddess. The female body is also the body of the vessel. The mouth is at the top of her head, and the spout is a kantharos held at its handles by the thin arms emerging from the neck. There are two conical projections with holes on the chest for breasts. The neck is adorned with a necklace in relief. The handle of the vessel is at the back of her head.

(110)

Grave Stele (112)
Late Hittite, 9th century BC
Maraş (not an excavation find)
(Inv. no 7694, H. 112 cm)

(111)

(112)

Two female figures are represented seated face to face at a table on high square chairs. On the table loaves of bread and a cup are seen. The figure on the left holds a pomegranate in one hand and a cup in the other. The other figure is shown holding another pomegranate and a mirror. They are dressed in long robes with a high waistband ending in a number of bands. Their outer garments reach from their headdress to their ankles. The name of the figure on the left is inscribed above her head as "Tarhuntiwasatis". Since the other figure is not identified it has been suggested that both figures might represent the same lady, alive with her mirror and dead with her cup.

Inscribed Stele of Storm God (111)
Late Hittite, 9th century BC
Babylon
(Inv. no 7816, H. 141 cm)

The basalt stele shows Teshub, the Storm God of Hittites, holding an axe in one hand and thunderbolts in the other. The disposition of his body, his attire and armour bear the features of both Hittite and Assyrian art. The inscription on the back of the stele is in Hittite hieroglyph. It was found in the 6th century BC Palace Museum in Babylon, and assumed to have been brought there by Nebuchadrezzar.

(113)

Column Base with Double-sphinx (113)
Late Hittite, 8th century BC
Zinjirli (Sam'al)
(Inv. no 7731, H. 106 cm, L. 167 cm)

The double-sphinx made of basalt would have once served as a column base. The deeply cut eye sockets obviously once held semi-precious stones for eyes.

Jar (114)
Urartian, 9th—7th century BC
Provenance unknown
(Inv. no 79.111, H. 31 cm, diam. 31.5 cm)

The jar may have served as an urn. It has a circular mouth with everted rim and a short concave neck. Its body is spherical and its base is slightly hollow. The body and neck were made separately and joined together with a supporting band of low rounded cover.

(114)

KADESH TREATY

The Kadesh Treaty (115)

Hittite Empire, Mid-13th century BC
Hattusha (Boğazköy)
(Inv. no Bo. 10403, 6549, 6674, 13.8 × 17.6 × 5.1 cm and 9.2 × 4 × 2.7 cm)

The battle of Kadesh, fought between Pharaoh Ramses II of Egypt and the Hittite king Muvatallish, and the treaty signed between the two powers after several decades, are among the most important events in the history of mankind.

In 1296 BC — Hittitologists and Egyptologists still speculate on the date of the battle and the treaty — the Pharaoh arrived with his army to the outskirts of the mountain of Kadesh along the Orontes river (today's Asi Nehri) and walked into a trap set by the Hittites:

> "They attacked the army of Re in its centre
> while it was marching unsuspected and
> not ready for battle. The army and the
> charioteers of His Majesty became faint
> before them."

After this quick victory the Hittite soldiers began looting the enemy camp. At this stage of events a new and disciplined regiment of Egyptian soldiers appeared at the battle scene and saved the life and honour of the Pharaoh. The battle ended in stalemate. After several decades, sometime between 1280 and 1269 BC, Ramses and Hattusilis III, successor of Muvatallish, signed a treaty.

The Kadesh treaty is known as the earliest example of a political treaty and written document of its kind in history. The original text was engraved on silver tablets of which there is no information. An Egyptian copy in hieroglyph survives on the walls of the Ramasseum — the mortuary temple Ramses II built for himself at Thebes — and in the temple inscriptions at Karnak. Nevertheless, the excavations of Winckler at the Hittite capital Hattusha in Anatolia brought to light a third copy of the treaty in the Akkadian cuneiform — the language of the diplomacy of the time. This is the treaty which is on display at the museum today. The tablet is broken, and the larger fragment has 45 lines, the smaller only 28. A much larger copy of this treaty produced by the late Prof. Şadi Çalık still decorates the entrance of the United Nations Building in New York City.

Despite the Egyptian and the Hittite texts being similar in substance they are not exact translations, differing especially in the priority each gives to its own ruler. However, when the texts are stripped of their customary eloquence in the Oriental style, one comes across with very contemporary conceptions such as: to refrain from offensive activities against each other, to enter into a defense against all kinds of enemies, and to return political refugees.

> "If a man — or even two or three —
> should flee from the Land of Egypt and
> come to the Greak Prince of Hatti, let the
> Great Prince of Hatti take him captive and
> have him sent back to Ramses, the Great
> Lord of Egypt. But if any man is sent back
> to Ramses II, the Lord of Egypt, let him
> not be charged with his crime, nor shall
> his house and wives and his children be
> harmed, nor shall he be killed or injured
> in any way, neither his eyes nor his ears
> nor his tongue nor his feet, nor shall he
> be charged with any crime... And as for
> these words which are written upon these
> silver tablets for the Land of Hatti and the
> Land of Egypt — whosoever does not
> obey them, may the thousand gods of the
> Land of Hatti and the thousand gods of
> the Land of Egypt destroy his house, his
> land and his servants."

The treaty concludes with the statement that its conditions will be honoured by the sons of the two rulers, who would succeed to the throne.

The treaty enabled the people of the Near East to enjoy a period of seventy years' peace, a very long time in ancient history.

(115)

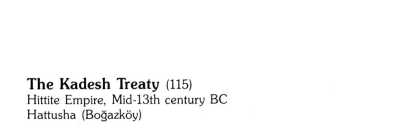

The Kadesh Treaty (115)
Hittite Empire, Mid-13th century BC
Hattusha (Boğazköy)

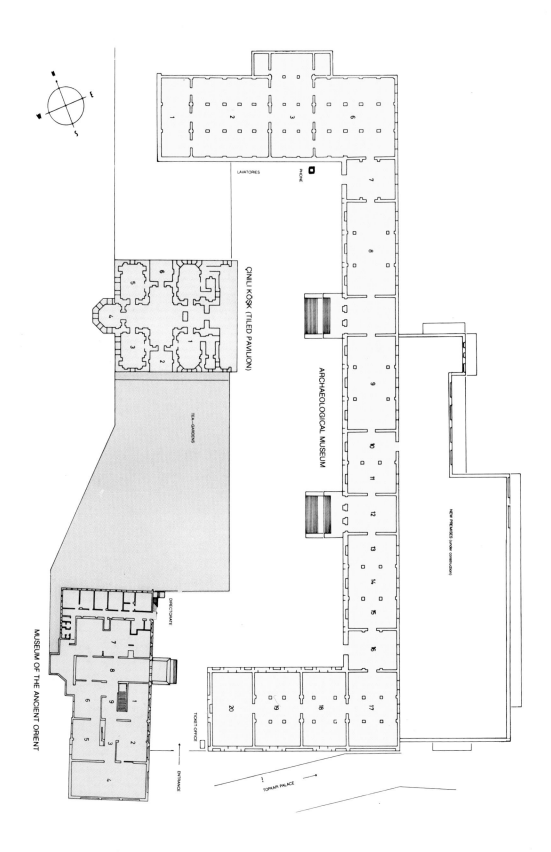

N
E
S
W

CINILI KÖŞK (TILED PAVILION)

5 6
4
3 1
2

LAVATORIES

PHONE

1 2 3 6

7

8

ARCHAEOLOGICAL MUSEUM

9

10

11

12

13

14

15

16

TEA-GARDENS

NEW PREMISES (under construction)

DIRECTORATE

MUSEUM OF THE ANCIENT ORIENT

7
8
6 9 1
5 3 2
4

TICKET OFFICE

ENTRANCE

20 19 18 17

TOPKAPI PALACE

PLAN OF ISTANBUL ARCHAEOLOGICAL MUSEUMS